My Little Book of
Big Trucks

by Honor Head

QEB

Quarto is the authority on a wide range of topics.

Quarto educates, entertains and enriches the lives of our readers—enthusiasts and lovers of hands-on living.

www.quartoknows.com

Designed, edited and picture researched: Starry Dog Books Ltd
Publisher: Zeta Jones

Copyright © QEB Publishing, Inc. 2014

First published in hardback in the United States by
QEB Publishing, Inc.
Part of The Quarto Group
6 Orchard, Lake Forest, CA 92630

All rights reserved. No part of this publication may be reproduced, stored in a retrieval system, or transmitted in any form or by any means, electronic, mechanical, photocopying, recording, or otherwise, without the prior permission of the publisher, nor be otherwise circulated in any form of binding or cover other than that in which it is published and without a similar condition being imposed on the subsequent purchaser.

A CIP record for this book is available from the Library of Congress.

ISBN 978 1 60992 924 4

Printed in China

Words in **bold** are explained in the glossary on page 60.

Contents

What are Trucks?

Trucks are big vehicles used to move heavy **goods** and **cargo** from one place to another.

⌃ The driver sits in a **cab** high up so he can see all around.

>> A truck's extra wheels help it carry heavy **loads**.

The cargo is carried on a **trailer** behind the cab. Most trucks travel thousands of miles (kilometers), but some trucks, such as forklift trucks, stay at their workplace, and don't go far.

⌃ Big trucks need very powerful **engines.**

Big Rig

A big rig has two parts—a cab and a **semi-trailer**—joined together. It is also called an **articulated** truck.

>> Two big **exhaust pipes** stick up from the cab.

⌃ Some big rigs have curtain sides, which make them easier to load.

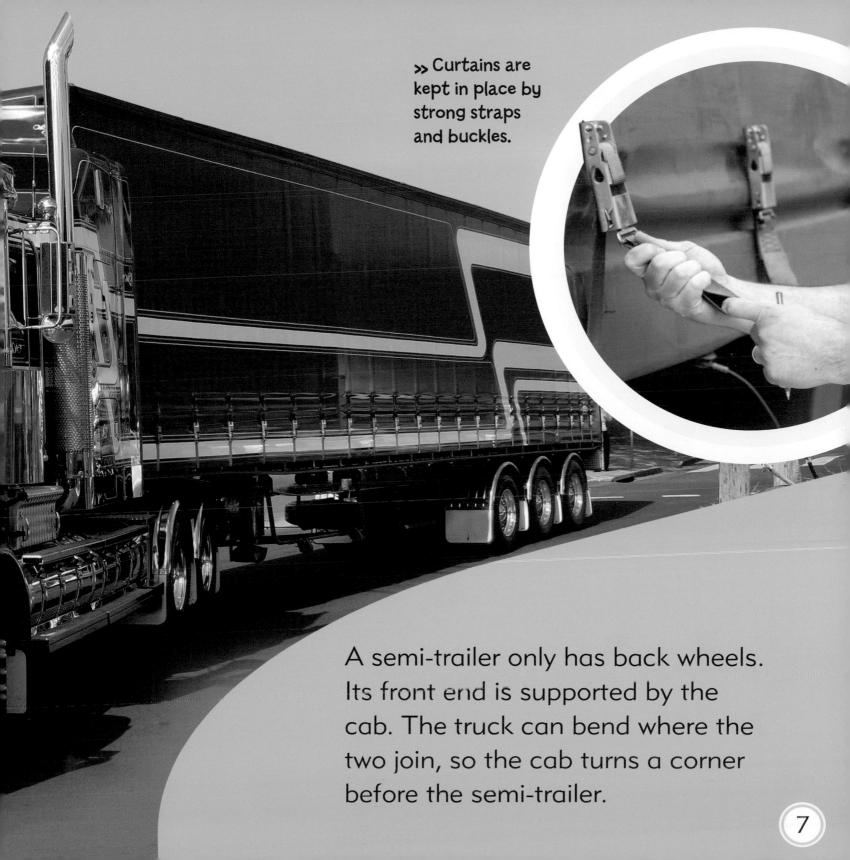

>> Curtains are kept in place by strong straps and buckles.

A semi-trailer only has back wheels. Its front end is supported by the cab. The truck can bend where the two join, so the cab turns a corner before the semi-trailer.

Rigid Truck

These trucks are connected behind the cab. The cab and the back are all one piece.

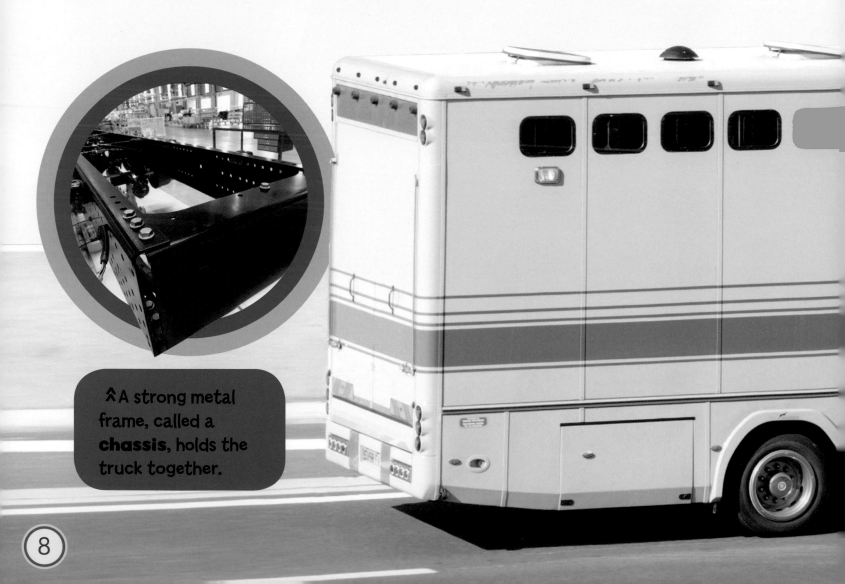

⌄This rigid truck is carrying horses.

⌃A strong metal frame, called a **chassis**, holds the truck together.

The part of the truck used for cargo is called the body. Its weight is supported by the chassis.

≪ The cab has a cozy sleeping space for the driver.

Road Train

A road train is a truck that pulls lots of trailers joined together.

<< This road train is carrying salt.

A record-breaking
road train was
112 trailers long!

Road trains travel
along the highways.

Flatbed Truck

A flatbed truck has a trailer that looks just like its name—a long, flat bed. This trailer doesn't have any sides.

« Spare wheels can be lowered and used if the load is very heavy.

∨This flatbed truck is moving a whole house!

OVERSIZE LOAD

Flatbed trucks are used to move goods that won't get damaged by rain or sun. The cargo has to be carefully strapped down to stop it falling off.

⌄ Extra-wide wing mirrors help the driver see past the load.

Tanker Truck

A truck that carries liquids is called a tanker. Tankers transport milk, oil, or gasoline.

≪ Liquids are pumped in and out through special pipes.

⌄ The tanker body has round sides, like a drink's can.

Some tankers carry a cargo, such as gasoline that could explode if there was an accident. The drivers are specially trained to put out fires.

˄ Tankers carrying dangerous liquids have a warning sign.

Logging Truck

Flatbed trucks are used to carry logs. They travel from the forest to the factory, where the logs are made into goods.

⌃The truck's **crane** arm lifts the logs on and off the flatbed.

⌃ Special tires allow the trucks to go off-road.

Logging trucks have tall steel **girders** along their sides. These stop the logs from rolling off when the trucks are driving.

⌃ These trucks often work in places that are hard to reach.

Auto Hauler

The biggest auto haulers, or car transporters, can carry up to 12 cars at a time!

⋎ Most auto haulers have two loading ramps, but some have three.

≪ The straps go through the gaps in the wheels.

Auto haulers transport new cars from factories to showrooms. Chains and straps tie the cars to the trailers.

≫ Driving a car onto the ramp takes a lot of skill.

276

Tow Truck

A tow truck, or wrecker, is used to rescue other trucks and cars when they break down on the road.

⌃ Strong steel legs stop the truck from tipping as it lifts its load.

A tow truck has lots of special equipment to help it remove cars from accidents, ditches, mud, or water.

⌄ Flashing lights warn other drivers of danger.

⌄ The truck has steel cables, a **winch**, and lifting ramps.

Concrete Mixer

A concrete mixer has a huge drum filled with sand, gravel, and water.

⌃Water is stored in a tank behind the cab.

>> The truck mixes the concrete as it drives to the site.

As the drum slowly turns, it mixes everything together to make concrete.

Concrete is used to make buildings, sidewalks, and swimming pools.

⌃ A **chute** is used to pour the concrete.

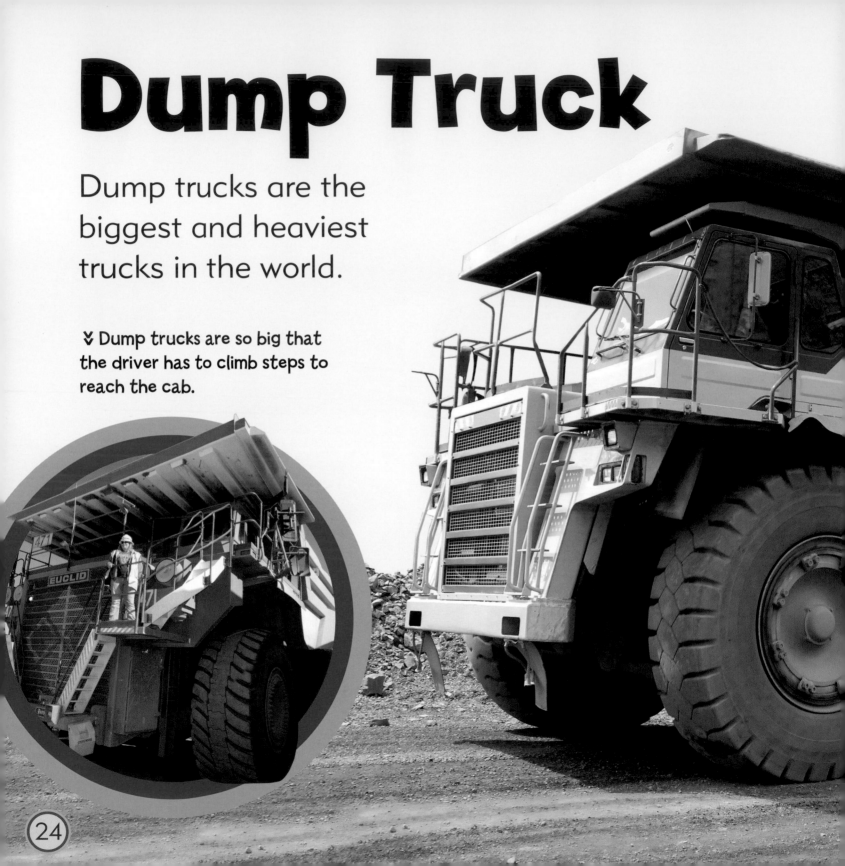

Dump Truck

Dump trucks are the biggest and heaviest trucks in the world.

⌄ Dump trucks are so big that the driver has to climb steps to reach the cab.

These huge trucks work in **mines** and **quarries**, carrying rock. The rock often contains valuable metals, such as copper.

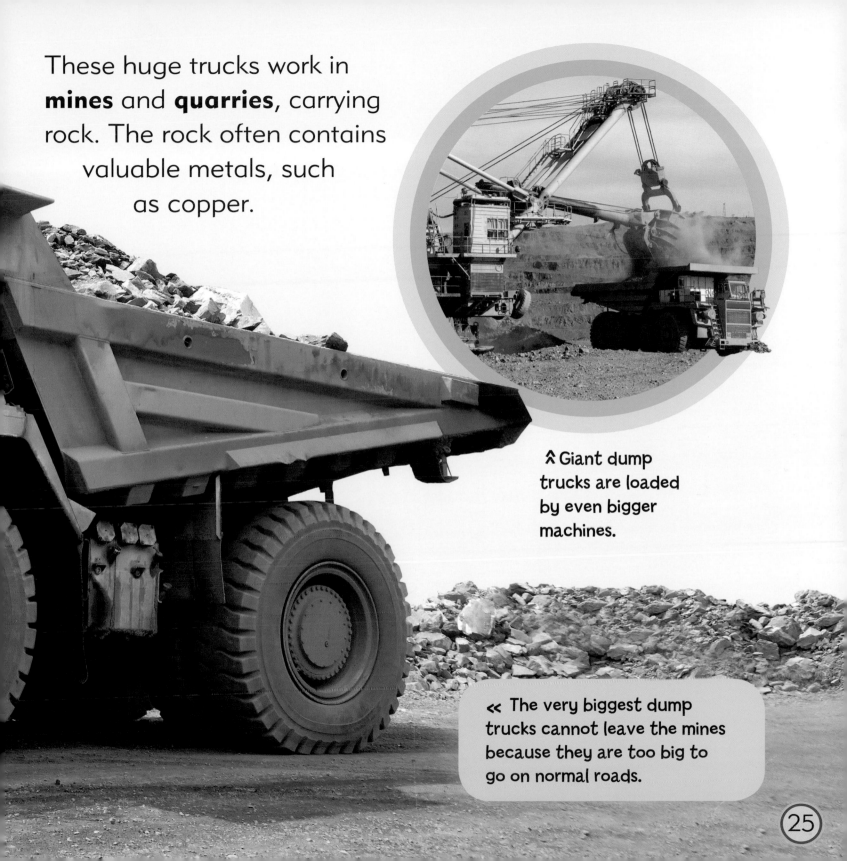

⌃ Giant dump trucks are loaded by even bigger machines.

« The very biggest dump trucks cannot leave the mines because they are too big to go on normal roads.

Tipper Truck

The body of a tipper truck tips up so the load slides off where it is needed.

>> The back of the truck lifts up to tip the load out.

⌃ Some trucks tip sideways.

Tipper trucks clear away garbage or transport loads on building sites. They are also used to move coal.

⌃ Some trucks have two tippers, so they can move even bigger loads.

Crane Truck

These trucks have a special arm that can lift huge weights. They are used to build tall buildings.

<< **Stabilizers** steady the crane when the arm is extended.

When the truck is driving along, the arm is folded down.

With its arm extended, the tallest crane truck can reach 47 stories high, and lift a load of up to 2.6 million pounds (1.2 million kilograms).

Each wheel is nearly 6.5 feet (2 meters) tall.

Digger

Diggers are also called excavators. They can pull up trees, scoop up earth, or knock down buildings.

⌄Crawler tracks work better than wheels on rough ground.

⌄ The engine is behind the cab.

Diggers are used with dump trucks to clear away earth and **rubble** in mines and quarries, and on building sites.

⌃ The bucket has strong teeth for digging.

31

Bulldozer

Bulldozers sound big and strong, and they are! These mighty machines are also called earthmovers.

<< A ripper at the back breaks up the ground.

>> The blade is used for pushing earth, sand, or heavy objects.

The blade at the front can clear forests or move huge mounds of earth to make the ground flat.

Compactor

This truck works on **landfill sites**. It is used to crush mounds of garbage, so more can be piled on top.

« The metal spikes on the wheels tear the trash and press it flat.

Compactors have special wheels to do their job. The wheels are huge, heavy, and spiked. As they drive over the trash, they break it up and squash it, so it takes up less space.

« The cab has windows on all sides so the driver can see all around.

« The blade is used to spread waste mounds into flat layers.

Drill Rig Truck

Some trucks carry a drill **rig**, which is used to dig deep holes in the ground.

⌃When the truck is moving, the drill is carried flat.

>> At the site, the drill is tipped upright for drilling.

Drill rig trucks make water and oil wells, and help build underground structures, such as tunnels.

⌃Stabilizers keep the truck steady when the drill is being used.

Loader

These hard-working machines have a bucket in the front for scooping up earth or gravel.

>> The driver uses a lever to move the bucket.

Loaders are used to clear ground or dig holes. They load earth or gravel into trucks, which take it away.

« The bucket scoops up its load.

» This load is being tipped into the trailer of a road train.

39

Forklift

This fast little truck is used to pick up and move bulky loads short distances.

↑ The driver can tilt the forks up or down.

>> The forks slip under the load to lift it up.

<< The engine is under the driver's seat.

Forklift trucks are used indoors in warehouses and factories. They are also used outdoors on building sites.

41

Robot Truck

Giant, driverless robot trucks have been programed to work in huge mines.

⌄ The trucks use **sensors** to avoid crashing into each other.

⌃ Each truck is as tall as a two-story building.

>> The trucks are controlled by a computer in space.

The trucks work in mines, but are controlled from offices over 900 miles (1,500 kilometers) away!

Tractor

Tractors are slow but powerful machines. They are used on farms to pull other machinery.

⌄ A hole in the back of the tractor provides power for the machine being towed.

⌄ This tractor is towing a machine that makes hay bales.

Tractors pull machines that plow fields, plant seeds, cut hay, and make hay bales. Driving a tractor takes a lot of skill.

↑ Some tractors do not have a cab.

Combine Harvester

⌄Inside the drum, the grain is separated from the stalks.

A combine harvester is used on farms to gather crops, such as wheat or corn.

⌃The spinning blades in the front cut the crop.

The combine cuts the crop, separates the grain from the stalks, and pours the grain into another truck that drives alongside.

⌃ The grain pours out of a long chute.

Truck Racing

Trucks not only do special jobs. They can also be fun to race. Truck races are watched all around the world.

⌄Trucks can race at up to 100 miles per hour (160 kilometers per hour).

Trucks of all sizes are used for racing. Drivers need to be strong to control their trucks as they race around the track.

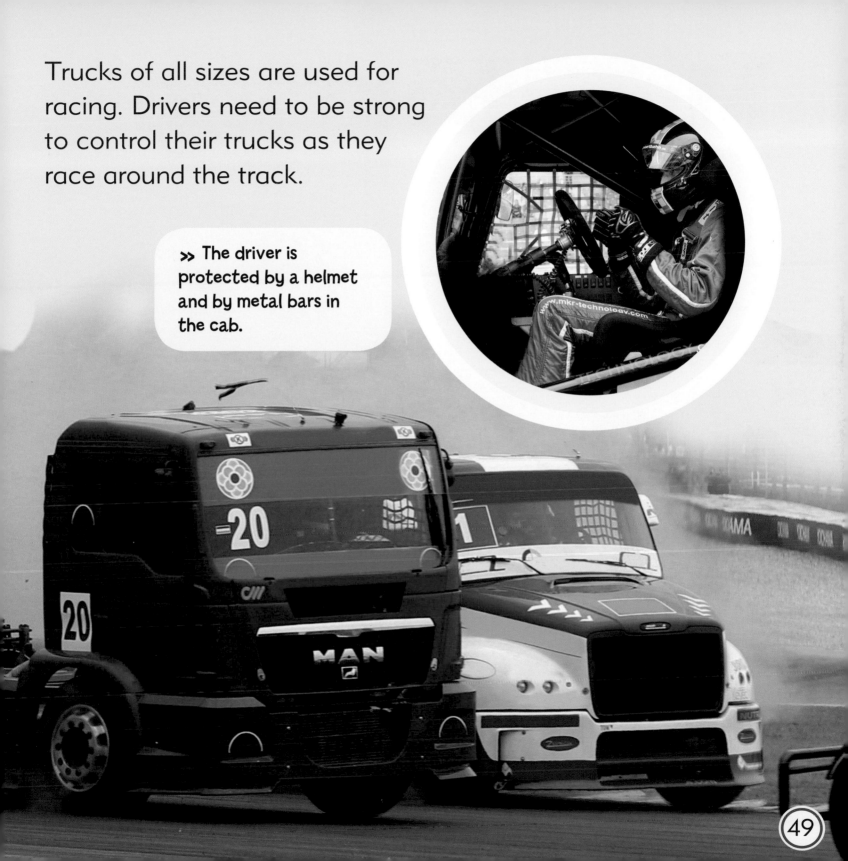

>> The driver is protected by a helmet and by metal bars in the cab.

Monster Truck

Monster trucks have a normal-sized body but extra-big wheels.

⌄ Car crushing is a favorite event at monster truck shows.

⌃ Monster trucks jump from ramps into the air.

These trucks are specially built to thrill the crowds at truck shows. The tires are often as tall as a normal-sized car!

⌃ Monster trucks can even do wheelies!

Pro-jet Truck

This truck has **jet engines** like an airplane that allow it to reach very high speeds.

>> Pro-jet trucks usually race on their own to see how fast they can go.

⌄ The driver wears a special fire-proof suit.

∧ Parachutes open in the back to help slow the truck down.

The pro-jet truck shoots forward from the starting line. It can reach a top speed of up to 150 miles per hour (240 kilometers per hour).

Snow Plow

These trucks save lives by clearing dangerous ice and snow from roads.

⌄ Snow plows push the snow aside.

⌃ Sometimes snow chains are used to give extra grip on icy roads.

Snow plows are used in countries that have a lot of deep snow each year. They help to clear the roads so cars and buses can run normally.

>> Some snow plows spread salt, called grit, on icy roads to melt the ice.

Amphibious Truck

An amphibious truck is a truck that can be driven on land and in water.

⌄ Tourist buses can now drive off roads and into rivers.

⌃ These trucks can move faster on land than in water.

<< This truck is used to rescue people from floods and storms.

Tourists make river trips in these trucks, and the army uses them to carry soldiers across rivers.

Record-breaking Trucks

From the biggest to the fastest, trucks have set some amazing world records.

⌃This 360 ton (326 tonne) Belaz dump truck is one of the heaviest trucks in the world.

The world's biggest truck is a dump truck. It is 65 feet (20 meters) long and 26 feet (8 meters) high.

⌃ The world's biggest tire is more than 14 feet (4 meters) tall.

⌃ The monster truck *Bad Habit* set the record for the longest ramp jump —208.61 feet (63.58 meters)—in 2010.

Glossary

articulated Having two sections with a moving joint between them.

cab The front part of a truck, where the driver sits.

cargo Something that is carried from one place to another by truck, plane, or boat.

chassis The steel frame that supports a truck's body.

chute A sloping pipe that things can slide down.

crane A tall machine used to move heavy objects.

engine Part of a truck that gives it the power to move.

exhaust pipes Pipes through which unwanted (waste) gases from a vehicle's engine escape to the outside.

girder A metal beam that supports a heavy object.

goods Items that will be sold in a store.

jet engine A type of powerful engine used mainly by aircraft.

landfill site A place where garbage is dumped and buried.

load A big, heavy thing that needs to be carried.

mine A place where coal or metals are dug up.

quarries Places where stone is blasted or cut from the rocks.

rig Equipment or machinery used for a particular job.

rubble Broken chunks of old stone, brick, or concrete.

semi-trailer A vehicle with back wheels only. It has no engine and must be towed by another vehicle.

sensor A small machine that can tell if something is moving close by.

stabilizers Metal "legs" that help keep a truck upright and stop it falling over.

trailer A vehicle with front and back wheels but no engine. It has to be towed by another vehicle.

winch A strong cable or rope used to lift or haul something heavy to a different place.

Index

Picture Credits

(t=top, b=bottom, l=left, r=right, c=centre, fc=front cover, bc=back cover)

Alamy
5tr © Dmitry Goygel-Sokol, 6bl © Radharc Images, 7tr © Image Source, 8cl © Alvey & Towers Picture Library, 8-9 (main pic) © Justin Kase zninez, 10-11 © Zoonar GmbH, 12-13 © Purestock, 18-19 © Justin Kase z12z, 19tl © Mark Fagelson, 19br © Jim West, 20bl © tom carter, 20-21 © Ted Foxx, 26bl © Oliver Pumfrey, 28-29 © ArtPix, Inc., 34-35 © David Mabe, 36cl © Mar Photographics, 36-37 © RJH_COMMON, 37cr © Backyard Productions, 48-49 © imagebroker, 52l © Patrick Phelan, 52-53 © JJ, 55br © Chris Cooper-Smith, 56cl © Simon Balson, 56-57 © Maurice Savage, 58-59 © ZUMA Press, Inc.

Corbis Images
8-9t © HEIKO LOSSIE/epa, 13tr © Barry Austin/Moodboard, 24bl © Douglas Keister, 50cl © Juan Carlos Ulate/Reuters, 51cr © Juan DeLeon/Icon SMI, 54l © Ocean

Getty Images
6-7 David Freund, 11tr John W Banagan, 12cl Comstock, 14-15 Lester Lefkowitz, 16bl Glen Allison, 16-17 Emily Norton, 27tr David Freund, 28bl Hazlan Abdul Hakim, 31bl Falcor, 34bl GeoStock, 42-43 Bloomberg, 58cl AFP

Shutterstock
fc Peter Albrektsen, bc tl WitthayaP; tc 11773606; tr Vladimir Melnik; c Vacclav; bl timothy passmore; br Natursports, 1c Scott Richardson, 2-3 travellight, 4bl R Carner, 4-5 javarman, 14l Marquisphoto, 15tr iofoto, 17tr Lisette van der Hoorn, 22tr 6493866629, 22-23 Blanscape, 23tr Christina Richards, 24-25 dragunov, 25tr Andrey N Bannov, 26-27 Andrey N Bannov, 30cl Kletr, 30-31 Vadim Ratnikov, 32-33 Dmitry Kalinovsky, 33t Girodjl, 38-39 Vadim Ratnikov, 39br Steve Lovegrove, 40tr ChameleonsEye, 40-41 KAMONRAT, 41br Baloncici, 43tr lexaarts, 44bl Marek Pawluczuk, 44-45 Rihardzz, 45tr Alexandra Giese, 46bl mihalec, 46-47 Kletr, 47tr casadaphoto, 49tl EvrenKalinbacak, 50-51 melis, 54-55 GTibbetts, 60tr Dmitry Kalinovsky, 63br Karl R. Martin, 64br Christopher Elwell.

Special thanks to the following for contributing their photographs:

Linda Bell 53t
Julie Giljam, Cool Amphibious Manufacturers International, LLC 57tl
Bridgestone Corporation 59tr